PLAYING WITH EMPTINESS

Collected Haiku

Ernest Sherman

In memory of
Leatrice Lifshitz

- haiku poet and
anthologist-

...her counsel,
encouragement and
example were crucial for my
poetic development

Thanks to my wife, Eva, for her kind and patient support, as well as her honest and penetrating reactions to my work.

Also, my sincere gratitude to Robert Milby and his fellow poets.
Their sympathetic resonance has been indispensable.

And, to the editors of Modern Haiku who supported me through the years.

And finally, my deepest appreciation for the recognition and publication of my efforts by Hayden Wayne.

Where did the haiku in this volume come from?

First, in teaching philosophy at Pace University from 1965-2000, I specialized in existentialism—that school of thought which stresses the individual and "becoming what you are" in full freedom and creativity.

This teaching taught the teacher to cross the line between all disciplines and relate to the world in its everyday concreteness. And somewhere along the line, I encountered a similar focus in the age-old wisdom of Zen Buddhism, namely to discover and live the sacred "suchness" of ordinary existence, because the Momentousness of things lies hidden in each moment—an open secret awaiting our openness to its presence. Which, brings me to haiku poetry—the great gift originating in Zen traditions of China and Japan, perfected by Japanese masters of the eighteenth and nineteenth centuries, and passed on to the world at large during the twentieth century.

For it is here that I found the magic of the Moment captured in two or three lines, whether in its serious aspect, or comic relief. (Technically, the term, haiku, is often reserved for the former, senryu for the latter.)

I hope the enthusiasm I felt in working with the form will be shared and co-created by the reader, for the spirit of Zen lies between the lines: between the play of speech and silence, foreground and background, fullness and emptiness. Thus, my title, PLAYING WITH EMPTINESS.

When the reader feels inspired to fill in the blanks with his/her own images and memories, the spirit truly comes alive.

May the Zen force be with you!

Ernest Sherman

- to the Moment
in all its
Momentousness -

My grandson and I
Shouting in the tunnel
Playing with emptiness

I.

Moodscapes

reddening winter sun
prisoner and guard
watching together

autumn dusk
white beach towels
darkening

all summer night
stars in the sky
stars in the lake

north woods night
the city kid drifts
with the galaxies

across the lake
moon on the mountains
mountains on the moon

waning summer light
a salt marsh whirlpool
swallows a cattail

ending my sweep
the spider's perfect work
caught in sunlight

in torchlight shadows
the cave wall bison
begin to breath

darkening cove
our canoe silently
fills the silence

autumn dunes
a faraway gull
follows my drift

as she chirps
the robin drops
a long turd

lawn bag
beside his sagging garage
leaves breaking through

warm spring breeze
the school windows open
to our drifting

early spring breezes
the neighborhood boys inspect
her billowing clothesline

cobalt, blushing pink
her new hydrangeas
a shade above mine

summer night
my turning in bed
the turning of stars

moved from the road
the caterpillar writhes
in my hand

going not going
swans slapping water
in winter slush

II.

People & Moods

art store window
through stinging sleet
glimpsing Monet's flowers

first frost
a torn letter
on the love seat

graduation film
looking back at me
looking ahead

first camp-out
eating from his shiny kit
a steak mostly raw

umpteenth charity
opening the envelope
with heart closed

august heat
the midway barker
loses his bite

late autumn pond
the dark ripples
return my question

cold winter sky
our parting words
even colder

the poet's lines
catching the November lake
leaving its silence

on the lot
my traded car
shining

first day
the strange, hard feel
of his school chair

retirement day
the professor erases
his last question

fiftieth reunion
the class bully
squeezes my hand

fiftieth reunion
the prom queen
friendly

reunion dinner
the class overachiever
in a shabby suit

where the shady maples
stood
the building sign:
"Shady Maples"

garage sale book
jacket cut off
in mid-hyperbole

rooftop Santa
waving above
foreclosure

III.

Deathscapes

speeding up and passing
the black hearse
for the time being

beside the arrow
to the poet's grave
other graves

sentencing day
the judge's black gown
sways on its hanger

last meal
a fly on the prisoner's plate
unmolested

death row twilight
down the block
a lullaby

on the funeral home
a large sign:
"Grand Opening"

recovery room
the nurse's voice
a little too soothing

prison sermon
the lifer made afraid
of the afterlife

graveside service
a cell phone chimes in
"Ode to Joy"

IV.

Warscapes

war games
a sidewinder crosses
the tank tracks

lilacs by the bridge
soldier after soldier
catching the scent

after the battle
blades of grass
righting themselves

the waves retreat
ribbon of kelp
on the rusted helmet

light raindrops
spattering his helmet
thoughts of the "real world"

touring Vietnam-
the farmer points the way
with a splintered crutch

Arlington-
the flag's unwavering
stillness

fierce thunderstorm
rattling his window
the veteran un-rattled

back at his car
the peace marcher
curses his ticket

village green
homeless vet camping
by the flagpole

battlefield reunion
the two sides
fighting back tears

last reunion
veterans facing
the casualty of time

V.

Witscapes

long Bible class
my wife and I
sneaking an apple

meeting in the lobby
the couple we avoided
our hasty smiles

showing her off
everyone talking baby talk
but the baby

first date
kissing
and missing

senior outing
in autumn heat
a pair of late bloomers

resolution day
replacing my raunchy calendar
with another one

meeting in the park
wishing that my old friend
had a name tag

office party
the receptionist becoming
more receptive

backwater hotel
on our bedpost
two mosquitos full-blooded

backwater motel
watching my flush
not flushing

election day
at the feeder
two blue jays ruffling
feathers

election day returns
two crows crowing over
a split pumpkin

election day defeat
in his garden
the candidate shows off
his prize tomatoes

marriage counselor
they enter
with hands clasping cell phones

yearbook shock
our class clown
a brain surgeon

terminal dread
the dying nerd
forgets the password

divorce court
his wife looks
pretty striking

divorce court
her perfume
comes on strong

over stiff drinks
his two ex's
share the dirt

black widow
a dead mate
on her website

my ex on the line
the caller I.D.
screws up her name

movie star's memoirs
her busy love life
without my part

Grand Canyon
tourists taking selfies
without selves

up there
billions of worlds
without my neighbor's dog

passing the trooper's car
a bit too fast
I look innocent

after the banquet
the French chef stops
for a Big Mac

swank restaurant
the headwaiter spies
my rolling potato

Slam! Dunk!
the awkward kid smiles
awkwardly

big trip
the hippie spaces out
on the moon voyage

the Big Bang
wherefrom? whereto?
who's asking?

Ernest Sherman began writing haiku in the 1990's and his work has appeared in journals such as Modern Haiku, Frogpond, North by Northeast, and Shadow Poetry.

He is the co-editor with Richard Gill of The Fabric of Existentialism, Philosophical and Literary Sources, NJ Prentice-Hall, 1973.

31975104R00062

Made in the USA
Middletown, DE
19 May 2016